JANE GOODALL

Pioneer Researcher
by Jayne Pettit

A Book Report Biography
FRANKLIN WATTS
A Division of Grolier Publishing
New York / London / Hong Kong / Sydney
Danbury, Connecticut

Cover illustration by Will Williams, interpreted from a
photograph by © Gamma-Liaison

Photographs ©: AP/Wide World Photos: 14, 101; ENP Images: 35
(Gerry Ellis); Gamma-Liaison: cover (P. Breese), 2 (Barry King); National
Geographic Image Collection: 23, 29, 54, 103 (Jane Goodall): 45, 57
(Vanne Goodall), 109, 114 (Michael K. Nichols), 17 (Robert F. Sisson),
9, 19, 26, 31, 40, 48, 61, 64, 69, 72, 75, 80, 85, 93 (Baron Hugo
van Lawick); National Geographic Magazine: 105 (Bruce Wolfe).

Visit Franklin Watts on the Internet at:
http://publishing.grolier.com

Library of Congress Cataloging-in-Publication Data
Pettit, Jayne.
    Jane Goodall : pioneer researcher / by Jayne Pettit.
        p. cm.— (A book report biography)
    Includes bibliographical references and index.
    Summary: A biography of the zoologist focusing on her work with
the chimpanzees at the Gombe Stream Reserve in Tanzania.
    ISBN: 0-531-11522-4
    1. Goodall, Jane, 1934– —Juvenile literature. 2. Primatologists—
England—Biography—Juvenile literature. 3. Women primatologists—England—Biography—Juvenile literature. 4. Chimpanzees—Tanzania—
Gombe Stream National Park—Juvenile literature. [Goodall, Jane, 1934– .
2. Zoologists. 3. Women—Biography. 4. Chimpanzees—Habits and behavior.] I. Title. II. Series.
QL31.G58P48 1999
590'.92—dc21
[B]   98-26410
                                                                    CIP
                                                                     AC

© 1999 by Franklin Watts
All rights reserved. Published simultaneously in Canada
GROLIER Printed in the United States of America
PUBLISHING 1 2 3 4 5 6 7 8 9 10 R 08 07 06 05 04 03 02 01 00 99

CONTENTS

CHAPTER ONE

DREAMS OF AFRICA

The tall, slender young Englishwoman sat perched atop a steep mountainous ridge, carefully recording the events of the day in her notebook as a blood-red sun slipped rapidly toward the horizon. Soon the area around her would be wrapped in darkness and she would have to wait until dawn to witness the first stirrings of the animals she had grown so quickly to love.

From their nests high above her in the distant trees she could hear the soft rustling of chimpanzees settling down in their nests for a long tropical sleep. Far below, the deep blue waters of Lake Tanganyika had turned crimson. The soft chirping of birds mingled with the muffled sounds of fishermen setting out in their boats for the evening's catch of dagaa, a fish similar to the sardine.

As the embers of her small fire glowed in the dusk, Jane Goodall tucked her notebooks away, pushed a strand of stray hair behind her ear, gathered her warm blanket around her, and lay back on the soft brush. The first stars of evening danced across the silent sky and then, quite suddenly, all was quiet.

The day had been a long one. For hours, she had climbed through thick stands of trees and trudged up and down the ridges overlooking the twin valleys below. Pausing occasionally to drink from the cool waters of the mountain streams, her eyes searched the rugged terrain for a sign of the elusive groups of nomads she had set out to study.

Following her arrival at the Gombe Stream Reserve, month after frustrating month had passed without a sign of the chimpanzees at close range. Gradually filling her notebooks with observations based upon indirect evidence of the presence of the animals—an abandoned nest or a trail of footprints—Jane continued her search.

> **I decided I would go to Africa and live with the wild animals when I grew up.**

Through binoculars aimed at the ridges across from the rock where she usually sat, she would sometimes spot them moving in a steady line through the dense growth. The groups varied in size and number, stopping to feed or to rest on the forest floor. Days were spent following them from

*Climbing into trees helped Jane to see over the grass,
which was sometimes 14 feet (4 meters) tall.*

distances of 100 yards (91 meters) or more. Attempts to move in closer sent the chimpanzees scurrying into the brush. It seemed as though the warnings of two acquaintances she had made before leaving England were true: "You'll never get close to chimps—unless you're very well hidden."

But Jane Goodall had come too far and had dreamed of this chance for too long to turn back. Years later she would recall her feelings:

> As I am not a defeatist, it only made my determination to succeed stronger. I never had any thought of quitting. I should forever have lost all self respect if I had given up.

Born in London, England, on April 3, 1934, Jane Goodall fondly remembers being taken on carriage rides through the city's beautiful parks. There, she could watch small groups of ducks swimming on the lakes and ponds. Insects, especially dragonflies, amazed her and she clearly recalls the tears she shed the day a man swatted and killed one that had been lingering overhead. Jane and her mother Vanne often visited the London Zoo, a special place for the blond-haired youngster who at an early age was fascinated with the creatures of the animal world.

When Jane was a little more than a year old, her mother gave her a stuffed chimpanzee toy which had been made in the exact likeness of Jubilee, the first chimp ever to be born in the London Zoo. Despite a number of predictions that the hairy toy would cause the child to have nightmares, "Jubilee" became Jane's constant companion. "I still have the worn old toy," Jane wrote many years later.

Jane's love of animals gave her mother more than an occasional worry. Jane was missing for five hours one day while she hid in a henhouse to find out how eggs were laid. The little "naturalist" lost track of time and arrived home to find that her mother and several others had been looking everywhere for her and had finally called the police.

In 1938, Jane's younger sister Judy was born and the following year, the Goodall family moved to the coastal town of Bournemouth in southern England. With its rocky cliffs nearby to climb and wonderful beaches to explore, Bournemouth was the perfect setting for a curious little girl to spend her childhood. On days when school was not in session, Jane spent hours combing the grounds surrounding The Birches, the big Victorian house where she lived.

By the time Jane was eight years old, she promised herself that when she grew up she would travel to Africa and live among the wild animals. Years later, after she had completed her schooling, she was working in London when she received an invitation to visit an old school friend in Kenya, East Africa. With her dream very much alive, Jane left her job and moved back to Bournemouth to earn enough money to pay for her journey. Living at home to cut expenses and working as a waitress during the busy summer season, she soon had her round-trip ticket in hand.

When Jane Goodall's ship pulled into the harbor at Mombasa, Kenya, in 1957, she was twenty-three years old and eager to explore the land of her dreams. She found it hard to believe that she had finally arrived in Africa after so many years of anticipation.

Second only to Asia in size, the vast continent of Africa is one of great contrasts and climates. From mountains and deserts (the Sahara is the largest) to tropical rain forests and savannahs (broad grasslands such as the Serengeti where antelope, elephants, and giraffes roam), Africa is made up of fifty-three countries. More than 700 million people speaking a thousand different languages inhabit this huge land. Great deposits of diamonds, copper, iron, and other minerals once drew settlers from Europe to make their fortunes. Big-game hunters from around the world wrecklessly exploited the grasslands in search of prized animal trophies such as lion and zebra skins, elephant tusks, and antelope horns. In the process, many species were driven to near extinction. Today, poachers (people who hunt illegally for profit) continue to rob the continent of its wildlife.

Unlike those people however, Jane Goodall had come to Africa to learn of its magnificent wildlife rather than to abuse it. As the visit with her friend drew to a close, she knew that she had to find a way to remain in Kenya.

Within a short time, Jane found work to support herself. One day someone who had learned of her interest in wildlife suggested that she go to see Dr. Louis Leakey. At the time, Leakey was the curator of the National Museum of Natural History in Nairobi, Kenya's capital. Dr. Leakey and his wife Mary were famous paleontologists who studied the fossil remains of creatures that had lived in Africa millions of years ago. The Leakeys were also anthropologists who worked to uncover the bones and artifacts of early humans.

In her interview with Dr. Leakey, Jane described her lifelong dream of studying animals in the wild. As she spoke, the scientist listened quietly and, to Jane's surprise, offered her a job as his secretary.

Jane loved her work at the museum and learned much from the members of Dr. Leakey's staff. Not long after, she traveled with the Leakeys on one of their expeditions to the Olduvai Gorge on East Africa's Serengeti Plain. It was there that the Leakeys later made major discoveries of the fossilized remains of early humans.

Dr. Louis Leakey holds the fossil remains of an early human ancestor excavated in East Africa. Many of Dr. Leakey's findings challenged accepted scientific theories about the origins of humans.

Before the expedition was over, Dr. Leakey spoke with Jane about the importance of researching the great apes in order to learn more about possible ancestral ties to the earliest humans. The scientist discussed his interest in a community of chimpanzees living in the remote forests of the Gombe Stream Reserve, bordering Lake Tanganyika.

Found only in Africa, chimpanzees inhabit an equatorial forest region that stretches from the west of the continent to the east. Those of the Tanganyika area are members of the Eastern or Long-haired group scientists call the *Pan troglodytes*. Dr. Leakey told Jane that little was known about the behavior of chimpanzees in their natural setting, unlike those in zoos or in medical research, because of the secluded places in which the animals existed. Only one man, Henry Nissen of the Yerkes Primate Laboratory, had observed chimps in the wild (in French Guinea, West Africa, in 1930) and that was only for a period of two and a half months. Leakey believed that was not enough time for meaningful research.

"There are all sorts of reasons," the great scientist explained, "why it's important that someone make a careful study of chimps in the wild. For one thing, it may soon be too late. [People are] rapidly penetrating and cultivating new areas, killing the animals and destroying their habitats. Details about the behavior of one of the most man-like creatures living today in its natural state may give us useful pointers as to the habits of prehistoric [humans themselves]." Dr. Leakey then asked Jane if she would consider going to the

Gombe Stream Reserve to study the behavior of the chimpanzees living there. "Of course I was wildly enthusiastic," she later wrote. Here, at last, was the chance for her dream to come true!

Jane returned to England while Dr. Leakey worked to raise the money that would be needed for the Gombe Stream project. After eighteen months, she was awarded a grant by the Wilkie Foundation, a group that sponsors scientific research. But there was a problem: For safety reasons, the government of Kenya wouldn't allow her to live in the African bush alone. Jane's mother agreed to go with her.

In June 1960, Jane and her mother arrived in Nairobi and began their mountainous 840-mile (1,350-kilometer) journey southwest to the lakeside market town of Kigoma, Tanzania. There, the two Englishwomen would gather enough supplies to last for a month at the Gombe Stream Reserve, meet with the game warden assigned to the region, and find an African cook to accompany them.

After about a week in Kigoma, David Anstey, Gombe's game warden, helped Jane and her mother load their equipment and supplies aboard his launch. Together with Dominic, their new cook, the group headed for Gombe.

As David Anstey's boat made its way toward the tiny shoreline settlement of Kasakela above which the women would set up their camp, Jane

A typical marketplace in Tanzania

felt her excitement mounting. Fixing her eyes on the dense mountainous forest that climbed sharply upward from the lakeside, she wondered what the next weeks would bring. Would she be successful in her efforts to find the chimpanzees?

Would she accomplish the task that Dr. Leakey had assigned to her?

The motor launch slowed as the group approached the settlement. Jane spotted several small huts that David explained were the homes of Gombe's game scouts. Further along the shore she could see shelters that housed migrating fishermen from other villages who came to the area during the fishing season.

Later, after unloading supplies and setting up camp not far from the game scouts, Jane found her binoculars and started out on her own. Pushing her way through the tangled brush she found herself climbing high above Lake Tanganyika, and discovered a troop of fifty to sixty baboons searching for insects and seeds. Suddenly, the area was filled with the frantic sounds of the youngest of the baboons shaking tree branches and stomping the ground. Older males in the group bared their fangs and barked warnings to the others. As Jane watched her initial encounter with animals in the wild, the baboons hurried off, vanishing over a ridge not far away.

After supper that first evening in Gombe, Jane and her mother happily reminisced about the day. Then, as she thought about her climb through the forest and the magnificent view high above the shores of the lake, she reminded herself that there would probably be disappointments

This 1963 photograph is an aerial view of Jane's first camp. (Lake Tanganyika is in the background.)

and perhaps some problems along the way. After all, she was untrained and unarmed in a remote wilderness that was totally unfamiliar to her. Remembering Louis Leakey's wish that she remain in Gombe for ten years in order to conduct an important scientific study, she privately told herself that she would remain in Gombe for no more than three years. At the time, Jane never dreamed that her research would continue for close to forty years.

CHAPTER TWO

FIRST SIGHTINGS FROM THE PEAK

A few days after arriving at Gombe, Jane and a game scout named Adolf, along with their porter, Rashidi, traveled into the thickly forested region of the nearby Mitumba Valley. Crossing a mountain stream, they began a steep climb to a higher elevation where Jane hoped for a better view to observe any chimpanzees that might be in the area. Along the way, Adolf pointed to a huge msulula tree heavy with ripe red- and orange-colored fruits. Noticing that the ground beneath was scattered with bits and pieces of fruit, Jane learned that a group of chimpanzees had recently stopped by to feed.

Piece by piece, I began to form my first somewhat crude picture of chimpanzee life.

Thrilled by the idea that the animals might be nearby, Jane suggested that they find a spot further away from the tree where she could observe the chimps without being seen. Suddenly a series of "pant-hoots," a term she gave to the breathy hootings the animals made to signal each other or to announce their excited arrival at an eating place, sounded through the trees below them. Straining through her binoculars, Jane saw nothing.

Then Rashidi spotted the first of the creatures and signaled to Jane. She counted them as they approached the msulula and began their climb toward the juicy fruit. There the group stayed, munching away for two hours as Jane and the others watched long, black hairy arms gathering the abundant feast. At last, the chimps began their descent from the tree and, falling once again into an orderly line, moved silently away.

For the next ten days, Jane and the others returned to the same observation area while the msulula completed its fruiting season. Each day, the chimpanzees returned to feed, their groups varying in number and in combination. On one occasion, the company was made up of females and their infants; on another, Jane sighted a gathering of males recognizable by their size (adult females are considerably smaller than the males).

*Jane Goodall took this photograph of an adolescent
chimpanzee and three adult males eating leaves
high up in the branches of a tree.*

On still another, an adult male had the entire tree to himself!

These first sightings, as wonderful as they were, left Jane wishing she could get closer to the chimps. How did individuals behave with each other? Did all females look alike and all males? Did they have unique personalities? Did they have feelings similar to human emotions? Jane hoped that one day she would find answers to these and many other questions that poured through her mind.

For weeks after the msulula tree stopped bearing its luscious fruit, Jane and her guides combed the dozen valleys of the Gombe Reserve without getting closer than 500 yards (460 meters) from the chimpanzees before they quickly scampered away. For days at a time, Jane was unable to spot a single one of the elusive creatures.

Despite her disappointments, however, Jane continued her search. She found satisfaction in becoming familiar with the reserve and the variety of fruit-bearing trees upon which the chimps fed. She learned to spot the wide number of animals that inhabited the 10-mile (16-km) stretch of land bordering Lake Tanganyika: bushpigs and mongooses; redtail, blue, and colobus monkeys; bushbucks; and baboons. The chimpanzees, however, continued to evade her.

Determined to go on with her study, Jane established a rigid schedule. Rising before dawn, she dressed in a khaki shirt and shorts, ate a banana, and drank from her thermos of coffee. Then, filling her pockets with notebooks and pencils, a compass, and small plastic bags for plant specimens, she looped her binoculars around her neck and set off on her daily journey.

Increasingly sure-footed, Jane climbed through treacherous bush and up and down the ridges and valleys. She learned to use the sturdy vines and underbrush to break a fall, and to crawl through dense thickets that barred her way. Often, her arms ached from thorns that cut deep scratches into her skin and her hair became entangled with overhead branches. Sudden rains sent violent crashes of thunder echoing through the mountains as she huddled, soaked and chilled to the bone, to wait out the storm. On clear days, the intense heat and heavy air caused her clothes to cling to her body.

After long hours in the bush, Jane would return to camp to record her observations and discoveries, no matter how small or unimportant they seemed. By the light of hurricane lamps she noted and described plant specimens she brought back with her, pressing them afterward between the pages of albums she carefully filed away.

*A mother chimpanzee and her baby rest comfortably
in their nest 30 feet (9 meters) above the ground.*

Once, when writing about an abandoned chimpanzee nest she had found, she recorded her
excitement in finding it to be a carefully woven
mat of leaves wedged into the branches of a tree.
To complete the story, Jane told of climbing up
into the tree and settling herself into the "bed"
to test its strength and comfort! Often, it was
after midnight before she finished her work,

turned down her two hurricane lamps, and crept onto her cot.

MALARIA STRIKES

A few months after Jane and Vanne established themselves at the Gombe Stream camp, they became violently ill with a type of malaria. A Kigoma doctor had told them that there were no mosquitoes in the area, so they had no drugs to fight off the disease. For many days, the two women suffered from fevers as high as 105 degrees Fahrenheit (40 degrees Celsius), drenched in perspiration as they lay on their tiny cots in the smothering heat of an African summer.

At times, Jane and her mother grew delirious and it seemed that the illness would never end. Night and day for almost two weeks Dominic, their faithful cook and guardian, watched over them.

When Jane's fever finally broke, she was eager to get back to work. She had been at Gombe now for three months and worried that she had accomplished so little in her study.

One morning, severely weakened by the illness, Jane packed her supplies and forced herself to climb a nearby slope to try to get a glimpse of "her" chimpanzees. If only she could get close to them!

By the time Jane had reached a rocky lookout spot, she had traveled 1,000 feet (300 m) above Lake Tanganyika. Exhausted, she sat down to ease her throbbing head. Minutes later, Jane heard the now-familiar sounds of chimpanzees' pant-hoots. Focusing her binoculars on the forest below, Jane watched a large group busily munching on the fruit of a large fig tree. From the rocky ledge where she sat, she could see every move the chimps made!

Having learned from the local people that the fig-bearing season would last for four weeks, Jane climbed to the rocky ridge each day after that. And every day, she spotted the chimps. As they traveled to and from the fig tree, the animals followed a path either directly below, or just above, her. Occasionally, they would glance her way as she sat quietly on the large rock she decided to call the Peak. Always careful to wear the same light-colored clothes and to avoid any sudden moves that would alarm the shy creatures, Jane soon realized that the chimps were becoming accustomed to her presence.

Day after day, the young woman filled her notebooks with descriptions of the chimps' behavior: how they acted while they were feeding, the ways in which they communicated with each other, and their curious habit of forming into new groups as they moved to and from the tree. Jane

A young chimpanzee enjoys the fruit of a fig tree.

also discovered that the chimps built their nests in trees near their feeding area and that they built new nests each evening. The young woman's patience, as well as her thoughtful respect for the animals, was beginning to bear results.

During the end of the fig season, Jane left the Peak and moved a little closer to the chimpanzees. At first, the animals scurried away, but soon there were moments when they would remain where they were—especially when she watched without using her binoculars. From her new spot, she learned to recognize individuals in the group. She noticed that, like human beings, they had distinct features that set them apart from one another. Jane began naming the chimps for familiar storybook characters she had loved as a child, or for a person she had known or read about. The first was Mr. McGregor, who was quite bald and reminded her of old Mr. McGregor in the Peter Rabbit books.

From her ideal observation spot overlooking the valley, Jane continued to name other chimps in the constantly changing groups. Before long, she had identified about fifty males, females, and infants. There was David Greybeard, noted for the handsome beard that encircled his generous mouth, Goliath, who appeared to be the leader of the entire community, and Flo, one of the oldest females, with her daughter Fifi and two sons, Faben and Figan. Gradually, as Jane began to notice certain behavior patterns, she could recognize John Bull (named after a feisty character in England's history) and Leakey, the sturdy, well-built male whose enthusiasm and energy reminded Jane of her inspiring teacher, Louis Leakey.

Each day, Jane watched the chimp groups, fascinated by the behavior of individuals as they

*David Greybeard sits with a handful of bananas.
His extended lips indicate that he has a mouthful
of food. The white whiskers around his mouth
are not a sign of old age; they appear on
young chimpanzees as well.*

communicated with each other. Once during a feeding period, she was amazed to see a female chimp move toward a male with her hand outstretched. "Almost regally he reached out, clasped her hand in his, drew it to him, and kissed it with his lips," Jane noted in disbelief! On other occasions, she watched two males greet each other with affectionate hugs, infants playing tag among the trees or tug-of-war with a twig, or just swinging happily from branches as they patted their toes.

Not long after, Jane made two incredible discoveries that changed forever the way ethologists (scientists who study animal behavior) think about chimpanzees. Both of these discoveries involved David Greybeard.

Sitting at the Peak one day, Jane focused her binoculars on a tree a short distance below her and noted a group of three animals—a male, a female, and her infant—sitting together as the male held something pink in his hands, "pulling pieces [of it] with his teeth."

There was a female and a youngster and they were both reaching out toward the male, their hands actually touching his mouth . . . the female picked up a piece of the pink thing and put it to her mouth: it was at this moment that I realized the chimps were eating meat.

As the three chimps continued to share their feast, a female bushpig with her young suddenly moved into the area, searching frantically for her lost piglet who had been caught by David Greybeard and was now being consumed.

For years, scientists had believed that the chimpanzee diet consisted mainly of plants and fruits, and sometimes insects or small forest rodents. Jane's discovery made clear that these remarkable creatures actually hunted and ate meat. (She would later learn that chimps engaged in cooperative hunting and sharing just as early humans did.)

The second remarkable discovery took place two weeks later. From a distance of just 60 yards (55 m) away, Jane came upon David Greybeard hovering over what she recognized to be a termite mound.

As I watched him I could scarcely believe my eyes. He was carefully trimming the edges from a wide blade of sword grass! I gazed . . . as he pushed the modified stem into the nest. He left it for a moment, then pulled it out and picked off something with his lips. The chimp continued probing with the stem until it bent double. He then discarded it and reached out to pick a length of vine. With a sweeping movement of one hand, he stripped the leaves from the vine, bit a piece from one end, and set to work again with his newly prepared tool.

Jane was thrilled by what she had seen. For years, scientists had known that a small number of animals, such as sea otters, were capable of using tools. The world-famous undersea explorer, Jacques Cousteau, and others had observed the clever little animals diving to the ocean floor to pick up stones which they would then use to break open their favorite shellfish. But David Greybeard had actually *made* tools to "fish" for termites!

Until this important discovery, humans had been set apart from the animal kingdom by the fact that they had learned how to make tools. Responding to Jane's letter describing the chimp's behavior, Louis Leakey eagerly wrote:

> Scientists . . . are [now] faced with three choices: they must accept chimpanzees as man, by definition; they must redefine man; or they must redefine tools.

About one week later, Jane watched as David Greybeard and his good friend Goliath fished at the same termite mound, scratching open a num-

Three chimpanzees take turns using vine tools to "fish" for termites in a termite mound. Jane's 1960 discovery that chimpanzees use tools revolutionized scientific beliefs about the differences between humans and other animals.

ber of entrances to poke their tools inside. She also noted that the two chimps picked several vines or stems at a time, trimming them and then setting them aside until they were needed. Jane knew this meant that the chimps were planning ahead—something that scientists had believed only humans could do.

News of Jane Goodall's discoveries spread rapidly throughout the scientific world. How was it possible that a young woman, without a university degree or training in the field, had made such significant progress in such a short time? She may have been untrained, but to the scientific community that had ridiculed Louis Leakey's belief that only long-term studies of the great apes would lead to an understanding of early humans, Jane's progress at the Gombe Stream Reserve was indeed significant.

Not long after, Jane was relieved and excited to learn that the National Geographic Society had awarded her a grant that would allow her to continue working at Gombe for another year.

THE BANANA ADVENTURES

After five months at Gombe, Vanne Goodall returned to England. Jane was alone except for the company of Dominic and his wife and daughter. But the long twelve-hour days were increasingly busy as the chimpanzees became accustomed to her presence. Many nights were spent at the Peak, her favorite viewing spot, where she kept a kettle and coffee thermos, small tins of supplies, and a blanket. As the sun set over the lake, she filled her notebooks with the activities of the day and ate a simple meal of beans and canned meat heated over a fire. Then, work completed, she would rest until dawn. What would tomorrow bring?

JANE'S PROUDEST MOMENT ARRIVES

After Vanne's departure, Dr. Leakey sent Hassan, his boatman of many years, to live at the camp and assist Jane with practical matters such as going to Kigoma for supplies. With Hassan and Dominic and his family for company, Jane was no longer lonely. The Africans were also of great help as she struggled to learn the local dialect of the Swahili language. In future years, as the number of observers and record keepers at Gombe increased, the ability to speak the native language would be of great importance.

During the months that followed, Jane was able to get increasingly closer to her chimps, whether at the Peak or along the thick forest trails that were the animals' ranging paths. Always careful to avoid sudden movements that might startle the shy creatures, she had learned that the chimps tolerated her presence if she sat down when they stopped to feed or to rest. She also discovered that the chimps felt less threatened if she avoided looking directly into their eyes if they happened to be glancing in her direction.

Then one day, an exciting thing occurred that Jane would never forget. She had been searching for the chimps for more than eleven hours, making her way up through the mountains and down into the valleys of the reserve without a glimpse of the animals. Now it was almost evening and within a short time the sun would be setting.

Pausing at the Peak for a rest, Jane soon heard the high-pitched voice of a young chimpanzee. Looking down on the slope below her, she spotted a small group of four chimps feeding on the freshly ripened fruits of a fig tree. Moving down the mountainside as quietly as possible, Jane watched sadly as the chimps noticed her and quickly disappeared. Then, much to her surprise two other chimps came into view not more than 20 yards (18 m) away—closer than ever before!

"All at once my heart missed several beats," Jane later wrote. The two adult males were grooming each other as they sat on the ground. Jane had observed the curious habit many times, and had come to recognize the grooming process as an important part of the chimpanzees' life. Eventually, she would learn that the action allows the animals to communicate their feelings to each other—sometimes showing friendship, reassurance after a quarrel, submission to an important member of the community, or even affection between two adults during courtship.

Writing about the thrilling experience, Jane described the scene:

Scarcely breathing, I waited for the sudden panic-stricken flight that normally followed a surprise encounter between myself and

Jane's observations led to the understanding that mutual grooming is an important social ritual in chimpanzee society.

the chimpanzees at close quarters. But nothing of the sort happened. The two large chimps simply continued to gaze at me. Very slowly I sat down, and after a few moments, the two calmly began to groom one another again.

After a few minutes, a mother chimp and her young peeked out at Jane from their resting place nearby, ducking into the bush when she noticed them and then shyly taking a second look at her.

"For over half a year I had been trying to overcome the chimpanzees' inherent fear of me," Jane explained, "the fear that made them vanish into the undergrowth whenever I approached. Without any doubt whatsoever, this was the proudest moment I had known. I had been accepted by the two magnificent creatures grooming each other in front of me."

Jane recognized the two males as David Greybeard and his friend Goliath, the mighty leader of the Gombe Reserve chimpanzees. She watched as each animal combed through the other's thick coat of long black hair, searching—not for insects such as fleas as is commonly thought—but for bits of forest debris or dried skin that seem to irritate the animals. (Often, a chimp will hold up an arm to show that he or she wants to be groomed.)

As Jane watched, the two animals continued for another few minutes. At the end of the session, David rose to his full height and quietly fixed his eyes directly on her. In that instant, she knew that the animal had placed his complete trust in her and that she had made a new and special friend. In the months and years to come, David

Greybeard would prove his loyalty to her again and again.

In her book, *My Friends the Wild Chimpanzees*, Jane reminisced about the special relationship that she and David enjoyed:

> I thought back over the years that I had known David, and of the major role he had played in the gradual increase of our knowledge. He had been the first of all the chimps to accept me, and his fearless attitude in those early days had done much to influence the behavior of the more timid apes.

Soon after this encounter, Jane returned to camp one evening to be greeted with Dominic's exciting news. A large male chimp had wandered into the camp that day, climbed an oil palm tree next to the main tent, and settled down happily to feast on palm nuts that had just come into season. The following evening, when Dominic reported that the same chimp had returned for a second helping, Jane decided to remain at the camp on the chance that the animal would reappear.

I remembered the day when David Greybeard had first visited my camp by the lakeshore.

The next day, Jane was thrilled to see David Greybeard enter the area, climb the palm tree, and settle down to the serious business of eating. Watching from behind the entrance to her tent, Jane could hardly contain her excitement. The animal was not more than a few yards away!

During the following week, David returned to his palm tree each day until the fruit supply had been consumed, grunting in happy satisfaction as he reached for each prized morsel. Then, after a short absence, he returned to the camp when another oil palm began bearing fruit.

Meanwhile, Jane lingered at her writing table for several mornings, making notes in full view of the tree, hoping that David would become used to her presence. Once, to her amazement, the chimp climbed down from his perch, crossed the open area leading to the tent where Jane sat and, with hair rising on end to show his excitement, grabbed a banana from her table. Staring in disbelief at the food that was to have been her breakfast, the young woman held her breath as David made off with his catch!

For months after, Jane and Dominic or Hassan left a small supply of bananas on the ground and David Greybeard became a regular visitor to the camp, munching contentedly while Jane took notes at her table. One day, she held out a banana to see if the chimp would move toward her hand.

Minutes passed as David nervously banged on a tree trunk and rocked back and forth on his feet. Finally, moving slowly toward her, the animal took the fruit from her outstretched hand.

As weeks passed, Jane made a habit of taking a few bananas with her on her journeys into the mountains. Many times, David would appear, take her offerings, and sit down quietly beside her while other members of the group stared from the safety of the trees.

"Even when I had no bananas," Jane noted, "David would come and sit beside me for a moment, with a soft 'hoo' of greeting." Having learned that the Gombe chimps uttered the same sound when they came upon relatives or friends, Jane was pleased by the compliment.

Soon, David's friends Goliath and the shy and sickly William followed him into the camp, watching from the thick bush while he consumed his daily supply of handouts. Gradually, they became brave enough to move toward their own treats.

"THE MOUNTAINS ARE AT THEIR MOST BEAUTIFUL."

Because of its location in the narrow strip of equatorial forest lying along Lake Tanganyika, rainfall at the Gombe Stream Reserve is heavy during

David Greybeard's excursions into Jane's camp in search of bananas became a frequent occurrence. Here, he gently nudges her arm in an attempt to get inside the box where the bananas are stored.

much of the year. From the "short rains" that begin in October, tropical storms occur daily, lasting well into May.

"At the start of the short rains," Jane once wrote, "the mountains are at their most beautiful, with twelve-foot [4 m] grass pushing up through the black volcanic soil, and flowers, many of them exquisitely lovely, appearing overnight."

Jane's biggest problem during the rainy season was the constant mildew on clothing, sheets, and blankets. Fresh foods quickly spoiled if not eaten immediately. Jane's equipment, including cameras, binoculars, and notebooks, had to be wrapped in plastic. Foggy lenses made it almost impossible to focus on her subjects. Travel up and down the steep mountain trails became difficult. Jane often found herself climbing trees in order to see above the rain-drenched grasses.

When violent storms erupted suddenly during the night, Jane learned that the chimpanzees waited out the rains sitting upright in their nests, heads and shoulders hunched against the peltings from above. During daytime cloudbursts, the chimps' behavior turned into frantic displays that the young scientist called "the rain dances."

One morning as Jane sat quietly beneath the branches of a huge fig tree while David, Goliath, and several females and their young sat feeding, the sky opened up and a deluge began. Wrapping her plastic covering tightly around her, she watched as the chimps quickly deserted the tree and moved up the slope toward the top of a ridge. Suddenly, one of the males rose to his full height with hair standing on end and began a series of ear-piercing pant-hoots as he raced down the mountainside and right back into the fig tree.

Other males in the group followed the first chimp, breaking off branches and shaking them wildly in the air or swaying back and forth as they, too, raced back to the fig tree. The storm continued to rage. Jane watched in amazement as the charging display was repeated over and over while lightning swept the skies and thunder roared through the mountainside. During the entire twenty-minute display, she noticed, all of the females and their young chimps remained in the trees at the top of the slope where the "rain dances" had started, their attention focused on the racing of the males.

> My enthusiasm was not merely scientific as I watched . . . from my . . . sheltering under a plastic sheet. In fact it was raining and blowing far too hard for me to get at my notebook or use my binoculars. I could only watch, and marvel at the magnificence of those splendid creatures. With a display of strength and vigor such as this, primitive man himself might have challenged the elements.

*During charging displays, chimpanzees scream,
bare their teeth, and bristle with excitement.*

Finally, the rains stopped, and the entire
party of chimps quietly disappeared from the top
of the ridge. In the years to come, Jane would
rarely see group displays such as this. Occasionally, a lone male might perform the rain dance by

himself during a storm, or become equally inspired when coming upon a waterfall. Was it fear that caused these remarkable performances? The answer remains a mystery.

On her journeys into the mountains, Jane frequently came upon troops of baboons or a bushbuck feeding on the grasses, but there were times when she had to move with caution through the soaked undergrowth. More than once, she spotted a solitary buffalo lying on the ground just yards ahead of her or a mountain leopard resting near the trail. At such times, she prayed that the wind would continue to come toward her, preventing the animals from picking up her scent.

"On the whole, I loved the rainy season at the Gombe," Jane wrote. "It was cool most of the time and there was no heat to distort long-distance observations. . . . best of all, of course, I was continuously learning more and more about chimpanzees and their behavior."

Toward the end of 1961, Jane's sister Judy came to stay with her in order to photograph some of the chimps. Jane's sponsor, the National Geographic Society, was eager for pictures of her chimpanzees. When the Society suggested that it would send a professional photographer to the Gombe Reserve, Jane balked at the idea. She believed that the presence of a stranger would alarm the animals and ruin the trust she had worked so hard to establish. Jane suggested her sister because of the strong physical resemblance between them, and the Society agreed.

Unfortunately, by the time Judy arrived at Gombe, the rains had begun. For the first several months, she had little luck capturing the elusive chimps on film. Finally, however, Judy's luck changed when she came upon a group of the animals fishing for termites with their handmade tools. In addition, a series of pictures illustrating camp life with Dominic, Hassan, and the others rounded out a fine collection that the Society accepted. They were the first photographs of the chimpanzees of Gombe Stream and served to introduce Jane's remarkable work to the world.

By the end of 1961, Jane and Judy packed up their camp equipment for storage in the village of Kigoma. Determined to prove her research authentic, and battling a scientific community highly skeptical of her findings, Dr. Louis Leakey had obtained permission for Jane to study ethology at Cambridge University in England. According to the arrangement, she would spend one term, or semester, at a time at Cambridge, returning to the reserve between terms. Along with her studies, she would share her findings with behavioral scientists at the university and accept a number of interviews with a British newspaper.

Jane hated leaving the Gombe chimps and the discoveries she had made, but she realized that if she were to continue her research in Africa, she would have to agree to the Cambridge program.

CHAPTER FOUR

FLO AND COMPANY

Jane Goodall later described that first departure from Gombe Stream as her "six-month exile." Although she was grateful for the opportunity to study at Cambridge, she found herself thinking about the chimpanzees she had grown to love. "What was David Greybeard doing?" she wondered. "What was I missing?" Finally, the Cambridge term came to an end and after speaking at two scientific conferences to discuss her research, she was on her way back to Africa.

Soon after Jane returned, she began taking notes on the way the chimps behaved toward each other when they visited the reserve or when they were traveling. One of the first things she noticed was that there appeared to be a social hierarchy, in which an adult male held authority over all others in the region.

During those early years at Gombe, David Greybeard's friend Goliath was the "alpha" male, or highest-ranking member of the chimp community. Jane found that when several of the animals visited the camp to get bananas, it was Goliath who reached for the fruit first while the others held back to wait for their turn. On days when she followed the animals, she would see chimps stepping out of the way when Goliath moved down a path, or uttering soft "hoos" when he came to join a group. Once, Jane watched as the alpha sent a female running from a nest she had just made for herself.

> The young female had constructed a large leafy nest and was peacefully lying there, curled up for the night. Suddenly Goliath swung up onto the branch beside her ... seized an overhead branch and began to sway it violently back and forth over her head. With a loud scream she leaped out of bed and vanished ...

In the future, Jane would learn that the high position of the alpha male in the Gombe community would pass from one chimp to another, and that each new alpha would have to prove himself by a demonstration of strength. She would also

*High above the ground, the 150-pound (68-kilogram)
Goliath feeds on the fruit of a huge tree.*

discover the many levels of social status among all
of the chimps—male and female—in each chimp
community.

For a while, Jane was absorbed in her observations of David Greybeard, Goliath, and William,
who had become regular visitors to the camp.

She noticed that David seemed to play a special role in his relationships with the other chimps and that he had calmly and completely accepted the humans who had come, uninvited, to live in his world.

Jane was fascinated by the fact that it was David, not the alpha male Goliath, who had first come into the camp. And it was David who had led Goliath and then William to the "banana patch." In his behavior toward the human beings around him, David was confident and relaxed, even mischievous. When younger chimps or the very shy William moved toward him in other parts of the reserve, he would greet them gently with his soft "hoo," and rest a hand on them in a friendly way or groom them briefly.

David had a remarkable relationship with the mighty but often excitable Goliath. "If I approached too closely," Jane later wrote, "David would reach out and lay his hand gently on [Goliath] or make a few brief grooming strokes on Goliath's arm. Such gestures always seemed to calm the more dominant male."

In August 1962, Baron Hugo van Lawick, a young photographer and filmmaker, arrived at the Gombe Reserve under the sponsorship of the National Geographic Society. A Dutchman born in Indonesia and schooled in Holland and England, Hugo van Lawick, like Jane, had long been interested in the behavior of animals in the wild. He had gone to Africa the year before to work in television film and had met Louis Leakey and his wife. Hugo later recorded the Leakeys' work at Olduvai Gorge for the Society and at Louis's suggestion, agreed to film Jane's work with the chimps at Gombe.

At first, Jane had been reluctant to allow a professional photographer into the remote privacy of her camp. Knowing, however, that a film recording the behavior of the chimps was important to the scientific world, she agreed.

The morning after Hugo arrived, David came into the camp for his breakfast of bananas. Armed with a camera, Hugo stayed hidden inside his tent, ready for a good picture. After a while, David finished and as he turned to leave, spotted the new tent. Curious as always, the chimp wandered over, lifted the flap at the entrance to look for more bananas and finding none, quietly left. In the process, however, a startled Hugo had his first photograph!

In time, van Lawick filmed the actions of David and his friends as they came into the camp. But working outside of the area proved to be much more difficult. Hiding behind a series of camouflaged "blinds" he and Jane had built out of the dense vegetation, Hugo would wait for hours to capture the animals on film, only to have them

*Vanne Goodall took this photograph of
Jane and Hugo at work.*

scurry away when they spotted a camera lens poking through the leaves.

Again, it was David Greybeard who convinced the other chimps that Hugo could be trusted. As Hugo and Jane moved quietly through the forest or up the mountain slopes, David would wander over to them in search of his bananas. While others in his company watched from the shelter of nearby trees, David would carefully inspect his two human friends to see if they were carrying his prized treats. Later, the mischievous chimp developed the habit of raiding the camp to hunt for a scrap of cardboard or a bit of clothing that he and his friends could chew on. Before long, other chimps were doing the same.

On one of David's visits, he was accompanied by an elderly female called Flo and her three youngsters, whom Jane had named Fifi, Figan, and Faben. "Flo became a frequent visitor, and we grew to love her wonderfully ugly features—the bulbous, deformed nose, the drooping lip," the scientist wrote later. Based on information Jane had gathered, old Flo appeared to be about thirty-five years old, with thinning hair, ragged ears,

> **We grew to love her wonderfully ugly features—the bulbous, deformed nose, the drooping lip.**

and few teeth. Despite her appearance, however, Flo had a gentleness and a warmth that had earned her a special place in the Gombe Stream community.

Jane quickly learned that Flo was held in high regard by both males and females. She was often seen in the company of several chimps, each of whom treated her with great respect, grooming her or greeting her with affectionate hugs. Old Flo proved to be an excellent mother—affectionate and patient with her family, and playful with little Fifi, the youngest of the brood.

Not long after Flo and her family became regular visitors to the camp's banana patches, she became sexually attractive to the males and brought with her a parade of suitors that grew in number each day. While Jane was delighted to be able to observe all of the newcomers, she soon found that the demand for bananas was steadily increasing. She asked Hassan to build a shelter to house a large supply of the tempting fruit. Unfortunately, no sooner had the "raid-proof" storeroom been built, than clever David Greybeard ripped a hole in its thatched roof, reached down, and pulled out an entire stem of bananas. In spite of the impish break-in, however, Jane and Hassan had a good laugh while Hugo's camera clicked away and the friendly culprit happily consumed sixty bananas!

For the next several days, Jane and the others worked to develop a set of closed feeding stations that would continue to attract the chimps to the camp, but allow each animal a limited supply. Time and again, their ideas failed. "Every type we tried the chimpanzees opened either by brute strength or manipulative cunning," Jane discovered. "They pulled pegs, opened catches, yanked cords. The adult males wanted everybody else's share for themselves . . ."

At last a solution was found. A series of concrete boxes with steel lids was constructed at several locations around the camp. Low to the ground but within view of the meandering chimps, they seemed to be the perfect answer to the problem. But it was not long before the animals maneuvered their way to the treasures within the boxes. They even unscrewed nuts and bolts. Jane was frustrated by her failures, but she came to realize that she had learned a great deal about the chimps' remarkable ability to reason and to solve problems. These characteristics, she noted, were clear signs of their highly developed brains.

During the time that the feeding stations were going through the trial-and-error period, Jane discovered yet another difficulty. Along with the parade of chimps, a troop of baboons began invading the camp. On one occasion when David, William, and Goliath were sharing a huge supply

Olly tries unsuccessfully to pry open a concrete banana box using a branch. Jane kept fifteen similar boxes scattered throughout the area to attract chimpanzees to the camp for closer study.

of bananas, a large male baboon charged at them in an attempt to race off with the fruit. William scurried into the bush while David ran for the safety of a totally relaxed Goliath who continued to work on his bananas. Then, as the frenzied baboon drew closer, David began screaming and thrashing about, only to run back to the protection of his friend. Finally, Goliath responded to the would-be thief by raising himself to his full size and giving out with an ear-piercing *wraa*, the chimpanzee's battle cry.

The confrontation lasted for several minutes, with Goliath pounding the ground and David screaming as he hid behind Goliath. The baboon continued charging, striking out at David whom he recognized as the weaker of his enemies. At the end, the two male chimps gave in and the winner ran off with what was left of the fruit. Hugo, meanwhile, caught the fight on film—a treasured account of the age-old combat between chimpanzees and baboons.

After three months of filming and photographing the chimps of the Gombe Stream Reserve, Hugo van Lawick's assignment with the National Geographic Society was completed. During that time, he had worked from early morning until dusk, trekked through the mountains and along the valleys through the heat of a burning sun, and shivered for hours in blinding rains to capture his magnificent subjects on film. Soon, this first collection would appear in *National Geographic* magazine, accompanied by Jane's description of her life with the chimpanzees. In the future there would be more articles and, eventually, books.

In the final days before his departure, Hugo succeeded in filming David, William, and Goliath as they worked their chimp-made tools through a termite mound. With this material, Hugo felt he could convince the National Geographic Society to allow him to return to Gombe.

DEATH OF A SHY FRIEND

In December, Jane began her preparations to return to England again to resume her studies at Cambridge. Leaving the camp in the hands of a young Polish scientist, along with Dominic and Hassan, she felt confident that her work would go on. But the departure proved even more difficult than the first time because the feeding stations had brought Jane so much closer to her chimps. During the months leading up to Christmas, she had filled her notebooks with the activities of old Flo and her wonderful family, and the antics of David, Goliath, and William. By now, she had grown to know the handsome Mike, who would one day become the alpha male of the community,

Four-year-old Fifi (right) holds her playmate, two-year-old Gilka. Female chimpanzees of Fifi's age play at being mothers. This prepares them for the time, beginning at age nine or ten, when they will produce their own young.

and Olly, Flo's droopy-lipped female friend whose little one, Gilka, was a playmate of Fifi's. Flo's current status as a sexually attractive female had brought into camp a number of males Jane had only been able to observe from a distance. Among them were the elderly Mr. McGregor, one of the first chimps to be named, and his young friend Humphrey. Other suiters followed, including Leakey and the wrinkle-faced Mr. Worzle whose tantrums were so childlike, and Hugh and Huxley—all with their own special characteristics and personalities. Throughout the months away, she would miss them and wonder what each chimp was doing.

Before leaving, Jane felt certain that Flo had conceived and she regretted that she would be absent during the endearing female's pregnancy. Fortunately, Dominic had agreed to continue the daily note-taking.

Jane's final observations were of William, the devoted friend of David and Goliath. For two weeks she followed the lovable chimp as he wandered in and out of the camp, struggling with a nagging cough that grew worse each day. Certain that William's illness was serious, Jane watched him carefully as he lay in his nests just outside the feeding area. As the days passed, the animal became increasingly feeble and unable to leave his nests to relieve himself. This, Jane noted, was extraordinary behavior because chimps are particular in their habits and keep their nests and themselves very clean.

William's appetite dwindled and he relied more and more on nearby leaves and vines that were within reach of his nest. On one occasion, Jane spent the night sleeping near the chimp's nest, and was alarmed to awaken in the middle of the night to see him drenched and chilled by a sudden rainstorm.

During the course of about a week, William stayed close to the camp, eating little and shivering violently as his coughing and wheezing intensified. Throughout that time, he seemed to take comfort in Jane's calm and reassuring presence, more than once building a nest right next to her tent.

On William's last visit to camp, he stole one of Dominic's blankets and sat down to munch on it. Soon, David ambled along to join him and for a short time they shared the cloth. Then, the two friends slipped quietly into the bush. William never returned.

CHAPTER FIVE

CHANGE AND CHALLENGE AT GOMBE

By the time Jane returned to Cambridge for another term, she and Hugo realized that they shared many things in common, especially their love of Africa and the joys of research and study. The two young people decided that they would allow themselves time to think about marriage.

At the end of the Cambridge term Jane and Hugo were married. After three days in London, they started out on the long trip back to East Africa. Much work lay ahead. The National Geographic Society had renewed its funding after a showing of Hugo's film of the Gombe chimps had been enthusiastically received. In the midst of all the excitement, Jane received a letter from Dominic announcing the arrival of Flo's new infant, a little brother for Fifi, Figan, and Faben.

Arriving back at Gombe in April 1964, the couple was treated to their first glimpse of seven-week-old Flint. Jane later recorded her delight:

> I can even recapture ... the thrill of that first moment when Flo came close to us with Flint clinging beneath her ... his small, pale, wrinkled face was perfect, with brilliant dark eyes, round shell-pink ears, and slightly lopsided mouth—all framed by a cap of sleek black hair.

During the next few days, Jane discovered that other changes had taken place. New chimpanzees were arriving at the camp for their share of bananas, young Melissa had become pregnant, and the inventive J.B. had figured out how to open the banana boxes. In addition to these developments, a number of the animals had begun to invade the tents in search of clothing, blankets, chair seats, and even wood to chew on. Some of the fishermen's huts had been broken into as well. Most startling was the news that Mike, one of the lowest ranking males, had begun to challenge the

The privilege of being able to watch little Flint's progress that year remains one of the most delightful of our experiences.

Hugo captured this photograph of Jane and tiny Flint reaching out to each other.

powerful Goliath for the alpha position among the chimps.

Soon after their return to Gombe, Jane and Hugo built new feeding stations about 1 mile (2 km) away in order to lure the chimps from the camp area. The plan worked well because the animals were accustomed to roaming the full length of the reserve in search of food. The new stations quickly attracted chimps they had never seen before and brought a greater variety of males and females to study. Eventually, a tent was set up in the area so that the couple could film and record the comings and goings of an ever-increasing number of the remarkable animals.

Months later, Jane and Hugo were thrilled to see Olly and her young, Gilka and Evered, making sponges out of several large leaves wadded together. They dipped the sponges into a tree hollow filled with water and then sucked on them, draining the liquid into their mouths. As time passed, it was learned that the chimps use their homemade sponges to clean themselves after a day of foraging, or to wipe blood from an injury. In future years, Jane learned that hostile chimps would use the tool to soothe a wound resulting from a fight.

One of the most exciting activities at that time was watching the infant Flint as he traveled with his mother, sister, and brothers. Soon, they were also able to observe Melissa with her newborn baby, whom Jane and Hugo named Goblin because of his resemblance to a little woodland gnome.

Although Jane and Hugo were now able to track the development of two chimpanzee infants, it was old Flo's attention to Flint that they most enjoyed. Flo, they learned, was a remarkably sensitive and loving mother. Long hours were spent with her new offspring while her two eldest, Faben and Figan, played nearby. Flo was patient with the ever-present Fifi who, like all chimpanzees, was fascinated by her tiny brother.

Flo loved to play with little Flint, tickling him and dangling him by a toe as she rested on the ground. Meanwhile, Fifi watched the antics, reaching out to groom the little one as he gleefully pant-chuckled with all of the attention and activity. Eventually, Flo taught Flint to ride on her back as she moved through the forest. At the age of five months, he was taking his first steps—with Flo's help. Frequently, she stopped to kiss him on the top of his head.

Flint soon learned that he was the center of attention. With the adoring Fifi always nearby, and his mother to watch every move, he grew increasingly demanding. He began to develop a fierce temper that erupted whenever he didn't get his way. In time, Flint's feisty behavior would have serious consequences.

GOLIATH FACES A CHALLENGER

In the complex society of a chimpanzee community, males and females each have a particular place. As Jane continued to observe the members

Flo was an attentive mother who doted on Flint.

of the Gombe Reserve, she was fascinated to learn that the chimps themselves were clearly aware of their ranking on the social ladder. As the animals wandered about in their constantly changing groups, feeding and grooming, building nests, or greeting members of the community that they hadn't seen for a while, the hierarchy shifted as individuals competed for position. In games involving young chimps, challenges between adolescent males, or contests over a female, the strongest, biggest or perhaps the most inventive chimps could win a higher place in the community. When aggressive behavior between rival males or females broke out, supporters of the two individuals lined up on each side. Social positions could remain fixed for months or change within a matter of weeks, depending on the relationships within the community. In the levels of the chimpanzee hierarchy, males were the highest in rank.

Goliath had been the alpha male at Gombe for at least four years. Powerfully built and a fast mover, he was the undisputed leader of the community. Then, in 1964, Goliath's position was challenged in a most unusual way by Mike, one of the lowest-ranking chimps.

Highly intelligent and capable of dramatic charging displays, Mike bluffed his way to the top of the hierarchy by the use of empty kerosene cans. He had begun his climb to supremacy shortly before Jane and Hugo's return to the camp, when his noisy displays sent Dominic running for his notebook.

One day soon after Jane and her husband arrived, Goliath and several other males were quietly grooming each other. Mike sat by himself a short distance away. Suddenly, the young male darted toward one of the tents. Grabbing two kerosene cans, Mike rose to his full height and strutted back to the place where he had been sitting. For some time, the chimp sat clutching the cans and staring intently at Goliath. Slowly, he began rocking back and forth, his deep brown eyes focused on the alpha male, his hair bristling with excitement.

Then, with a menacing glare Mike stood up and started hooting wildly as he charged toward the group, kicking the kerosene cans in front of him as he ran. Goliath and his friends scurried up the trees, screaming and swinging frantically from branch to branch.

Minutes later, all was quiet. Mike, who had stormed off into the bush, was nowhere to be seen. After a while, the chimps climbed down from the trees, glancing about the area cautiously as they moved back to where they had been sitting. But just as they settled down to continue their grooming, the sounds of Mike's pant-hoots rang through the bush. Charging toward Goliath and the oth-

*Mike throws one of the empty kerosene cans.
Chimpanzees dislike loud noises. As a result of
the racket Mike made with the cans, the other
chimpanzees began to show him more respect.*

ers, the chimp set up a terrible noise, knocking
the tin cans over and over again along the ground.
For a second time, the older chimps scattered.

By now exhausted and out of breath, Mike sat
down to rest. Within a short time, five of the

males returned, one by one, to greet the younger chimp submissively, bending low and kissing him on his thigh. David Greybeard arrived to lay a supportive hand on Mike while the others started grooming him to show their respect. Goliath, however, kept his distance—concentrating his gaze on Mike—aware by now that his position as alpha male was being challenged. Jane later wrote about Mike's stunning performance, noting that "it seemed that Mike actually planned his charging displays; almost, one might say, in cold blood."

During the following weeks, Mike continued his threats against Goliath, lashing out at the alpha male at every opportunity. His displays grew more violent when he discovered how to toss the kerosene cans into the air, once hitting Jane in the head when she was caught between the two. Finally, having filmed as much of the action as they dared, Hugo and Jane began removing the cans from the area. Mike then began attacking Hugo's equipment. In one of his most destructive displays, the animal actually overturned a supply cabinet, sending its contents crashing to the ground.

For many months the tension between Mike and Goliath continued to build as the two fought for control of the Gombe community. And then for some strange reason, Goliath left the camp. All was peaceful in the community and Mike began to enjoy his new role as the alpha male.

But after two weeks, Goliath suddenly reappeared—his familiar pant-hoot greeting echoing through the trees as he approached the camp. Mike picked up the sounds and immediately was alert. Returning Goliath's call, he raced up a tree and stationed himself on a branch, the hair on his body rising slowly.

Goliath stepped from the bush brandishing a branch and charged toward the tree where Mike sat. With a giant leap, Goliath reached the top of a nearby tree and waited silently for a response. Mike began rattling branches and dropping to the ground to reach for rocks to hurl. Not satisfied, he charged into Goliath's tree and the two rattled branches at each other in threatening displays of strength.

For close to thirty minutes, the two animals outdid one another in acrobatic endeavors. And then to Jane's amazement, the frantic activity stopped. Goliath crossed over to Mike, huddled submissively, and began to groom him. A moment later, Mike returned the compliment and there the animals sat—grooming each other for more than an hour.

That was the last real duel between the two males. From then on, it seemed that

Goliath accepted Mike's superiority, and a strangely intense relationship grew up between the two. They often greeted one another with much display of emotion, embracing or patting one another, kissing each other in the neck . . .

DISEASE INVADES THE CAMP

That same year (1964), realizing that their research at Gombe had expanded to the point where it was more than two people could handle, Jane and Hugo employed Edna Koning, a young woman who had read about their work and wanted to join them. Edna's assistance saved Jane the painstaking labor of handwritten note-taking, since she could now record her observations during the day and turn the tapes over to Edna to type in the evening.

Jane and Hugo continued to work from dawn to dusk, returning either to the newly established Ridge camp where the banana stations were located, or to Jane's original lakeside camp. At night, while Hugo developed his film or worked on their accounts, Jane concentrated on her Ph.D. thesis.

Vanne Goodall rejoined the group during a visit later that year to lend a hand with all of the data, files, and charts that were fast accumulating. Soon, however, it was necessary to employ a second assistant to share the increasingly heavy work load, making it possible for Jane to spend longer periods "following," as she called her explorations throughout the Gombe Reserve.

Week by week, the number of chimps visiting the Ridge camp steadily increased. By now there were at least forty-five animals, including Flo and her family, David Greybeard, Leakey, and others from the original group. Gradually however, as the chimps became increasingly trustful, problems began to develop as they wandered about the area.

Early one morning, David invaded Vanne's tent and engaged in a tug-of-war with her for her pajamas as she struggled to get dressed. On another occasion, Rodolf, a large male known for his stone-throwing talents, sidled up to Jane and grabbed at her shirt in an attempt to rip off a piece to chew. Another situation involved Fifi, old Flo's mischievous daughter, who reached into Jane's pocket one day with a freshly made tool to spear a banana. After an unsuccessful attempt, she tagged along behind, making pathetic little sounds until Jane surrendered what was to have been her lunch. And then there was the time Mr. McGregor made off with four prized hard-boiled eggs, thinking they were raw (such as those in birds' nests). Much to his surprise they were not what he expected—and they were hot, too!

*Jane gives bananas to David Greybeard during
one of his many visits to camp.*

Fortunately for Jane and Hugo, the National
Geographic Society continued to award them the
funds necessary to continue their research. In
1965, the organization made possible the first per-

manent buildings, allowing space for a small office, bedrooms, and a kitchen. A second structure served as private living quarters for the young couple.

Soon after the work was completed, Jane had to return to Cambridge to complete her Ph.D. and Hugo was off to a new filming assignment. Their two assistants remained at the reserve to continue the observations and answer requests from students wanting to join the Gombe team. Soon, the first of these would arrive to spend a year or more studying chimpanzee behavior.

In 1966, tragedy struck the Gombe Reserve. The first sign that things were not as they should be happened when Jane noticed that a four-week-old baby born to Olly, Flo's devoted friend, was ill. Olly had come into camp to feed on bananas and as she carried the baby, the little one's arms and legs seemed unusually limp. Olly's daughter Gilka was also present, and as she reached out to touch the infant's hands there was no response.

When Olly returned the following day, the baby screamed in pain with every movement that its mother made. By now, its arms and legs were lifeless and Gilka—perhaps sensing that something was terribly wrong—hovered close by but didn't try to touch it.

A short time later, Jane followed Olly and the baby and Gilka out of the camp as they moved into the valley below. Jane watched as the family stopped to rest, Olly cradling her infant and taking care to fold its limp little arms and legs onto her lap.

After several attempts to continue along the path, the mother finally climbed a tree and settled down with the baby in her arms. Gilka sat beside her, grooming her mother and staring at her sibling. Suddenly, the clouds burst overhead, and Jane struggled to see the three as they huddled against the storm.

By the time the rain had stopped, the baby was silent. When Olly climbed down from the tree, Jane could see that the infant was dead.

The next day, Olly and Gilka returned to the camp to feed. The dead little chimp lay on its mother's back, dropping to the ground now and again as Olly and her daughter ate. A number of other chimps and a baboon or two came close to view the sad sight. Olly paid no attention as she sat staring straight ahead, her body hunched over the dead infant.

Their meal over, the mother and daughter wandered off again with Jane following. Hours later, after a long journey through the tropical forest and tangled bush, Jane left the chimps and returned to the camp with a recording of her observations. Among these, she had noted Gilka's attempts to play with the dead infant and finally to pick it up and hold it close to her. Olly meanwhile, had sat staring into space—seeming to grieve—for her lost child.

It would be weeks before Jane and the others learned that an outbreak of polio had occurred in the Kigoma area, affecting many of the Africans living there. The crippling disease had spread to within 10 miles (16 km) of Gombe and had struck a number of chimpanzees that had been feeding along the outskirts there.

Hearing the news, Jane spent anxious hours waiting for a plane to arrive from Nairobi with vaccines for everyone and for as many chimps as they could save. Jane was particularly concerned because she was now pregnant.

Once she and the others had taken the vaccine, the difficult work of injecting the chimps' bananas with the required dosage began. For months, care had to be taken to make certain that each animal that arrived at the camp had received its medicine and that none had received more than was needed.

"I think those few months were the darkest I have ever lived through," Jane would write. "Every time a chimp stopped visiting the feeding area, we started wondering whether we would ever see him again, or, worse, if he would reappear hideously crippled."

By the time the crisis had passed, six of the Gombe Stream chimpanzees had died and nine had become paralyzed in some way. Melissa's neck and shoulders had been affected, and Flo's son Faben and another young male each lost the use of an arm. One poor creature struggled to find food without the use of either arm. Realizing that the animal was slowly starving to death, Jane and Hugo came to the reluctant decision that he had to be shot.

"And there were other victims—like fat, bustling J.B., of whom we had all become so fond," Jane would later comment, "who just disappeared, and we could only [guess] about their lonely deaths."

One of the last chimps to be stricken with polio was the wonderfully high-spirited Mr. McGregor. Noticing Flo, Fifi, and little Flint acting strangely one night, Jane and Hugo followed them only to discover Mr. McGregor dragging his paralyzed legs toward a low bush laden with fruit. When he had consumed all of the berries in one spot, he would use his powerful arms to edge himself forward or backward to reach another supply.

After the other chimps had ambled off into the night, Jane and her husband watched Mr. McGregor pull himself along in search of a low-branched tree where he could build a nest. Finding one at last, the poor animal dragged his dead limbs onto it, and struggled with the makings of a

*Jane developed such a remarkable trust with so many
of the chimpanzees that close encounters like this
one became common. But the strong bond among
them made the loss of those stricken with polio
even more difficult to accept.*

nest. For more than a week, Mr. McGregor's condition remained the same. Exhausted by the effort to move from place to place, the animal left his nest only to feed.

"We kept hoping to notice some flicker of life return to his paralyzed legs," Jane wrote, "but he never twitched as much as a toe."

Finally, concerned that Mr. McGregor was not getting enough food, Jane and Hugo began weaving crude baskets out of leaves that they packed with bananas and other fruit and left near the animal's nest. Jane even managed to drip water into Mr. McGregor's mouth once he came to trust her help.

As the old chimp grew steadily weaker, the other animals, frightened by his behavior, stayed away from him. Only the feisty Humphrey remained nearby, as if to give the sick animal a bit of company.

In one of the most difficult recordings Jane had to make during that sad time, she described an incident involving a group of chimps that were grooming each other in a tree not far from where Mr. McGregor was resting.

Mutual grooming normally takes up a good deal of a chimpanzee's time, and the old male had been drastically starved of this important social contact since his illness.

While the session continued, Mr. McGregor watched longingly from his nest. Finally, with great effort, he lowered himself to the ground and struggled over to where the chimps sat.

With a loud grunt of pleasure he reached a hand toward them in greeting—but even before he made contact they both had swung quickly away and without a backward glance started grooming on the far side of the tree. For a full two minutes old Gregor sat motionless, staring after them.

After Mr. McGregor badly injured an arm in his effort to move about, Jane and her husband knew they could not let him suffer any longer. The next morning Mr. McGregor was fed his favorite food—raw eggs—and relieved of his misery. For six months, his faithful friend Humphrey returned again and again to the tree where Mr. McGregor had built his last nest. He would stay there for the longest time, looking out over the valleys and the ridges that he and his old companion had once roamed together, as if hoping that someday he might return.

CHAPTER SIX

ALMOST HUMAN?

In her book, *Through a Window*, Jane Goodall
wrote, "Louis Leakey sent me to Gombe in the
hope that a better understanding of the behavior
of our closest relatives would provide a new window onto our own past."

Now, almost forty years later, the results of
her patient and courageous research of the chimpanzees of Gombe Stream has indeed opened
many windows. This research, which represents
the longest single study of an animal species in
the wild, has enriched our understanding of these
fascinating creatures.

Since 1960 when she began her work, Jane
has observed generations of chimps as they wandered through the forests, ridges, and valleys, living side by side in their complex communities,
raising their young and battling diseases.

Little did Jane know that day when she first stepped onto the shores of Lake Tanganyika that she would continue her study decades longer than Louis Leakey's initial request that she remain at Gombe for ten years. At that time, she would have found it hard to believe that she would turn the scientific community upside down, erasing previously held notions about the way chimps live in the wild. Jane's discoveries have led to a better understanding of these highly intelligent animals and of the many ways in which chimpanzees and humans are similar.

> The affectionate, supportive and enduring bonds between family members, the long period of childhood dependency, the importance of learning, non-verbal communication . . . tool-using and tool-making [and] similarities in the structure of the brain and central nervous system . . . [have] been helpful to those studying early man. . . .

In fact, the DNA genetic makeup of chimpanzees and humans differs by less than two percent! Yet, as Dr. Goodall would remind us today, our two species are "eons apart," particularly in the way that humans communicate by the use of a verbal language.

By 1964, when Jane realized that she needed assistants to help with her research, the Gombe Stream Research Centre was established. Once more, the National Geographic Society stepped in to provide funding for two graduate students to continue Jane's work while she was away at Cambridge. Later, in cooperation with California's Stanford University, many more students joined the center. "So it was that the Gombe Stream Research Centre was conceived," Jane noted. "I had no idea at the time that it was to become one of the best-known field stations in the world."

Then in 1967 as the work broadened, the Gombe Reserve became the Gombe National Park, under the direction of the Tanzania National Parks System. This gave Jane and the others added protection from poachers eager to capture infant chimps for resale to exploiters. A crew of park rangers set up stations throughout the area and the African staff expanded, building quarters along the lake and working with Dominic, Has-

For chimpanzees, whose brains are more like those of humans than are those of any other living animal ... early experience may have a profound effect on adult behavior.

san, and Rashidi, the guide who had introduced Jane to the magnificence of the reserve.

As Jane's work continued, she learned that chimpanzees move through many stages of development, much as humans do. She noted that infants from birth to age five are totally dependent upon their mothers. For the next two years, the youngsters begin to make their own nests and travel on their own. Adolescent males from about eight to twelve are increasingly independent and like to travel with adult males. Females of the same age stay close to their mothers and siblings. Male chimps between thirteen and fifteen spend most of their time with adult males and try to dominate adult females. Females of about that age continue their close ties with their mothers and can become pregnant. (Pregnant females carry their young for eight months and rarely bear more than one infant at a time.) At maturity, males compete for social status, spend much time with other males, and wander throughout the home range. Mature females spend a lot of time raising their offspring and enjoying the companionship of other females and their young. Elderly chimps from thirty-three years to death lose a considerable amount of hair and often move about by themselves. Teeth become loose or worn down.

Throughout these stages of development, Jane discovered, the ever-changing groups that travel together communicate through a variety of non-verbal sounds that range from little contented "greeting grunts" to pant-grunts, screams, or the highly excited *wraas* uttered during aggressive behavior.

Chimps also communicate through touch, showing submission to a higher-ranking adult, or affectionate hand-holding, embracing, and kissing. Frequent grooming sessions throughout the day can signal reassurance, submission, or even apology.

Jane found that chimpanzees, like humans, indicate their feelings by any number of facial expressions. When a male chimp presses his lips into a tight, rigid line he is showing that he is ready for a display or a confrontation with another animal. (Picture this kind of expression on Mike's face as he banged his kerosene cans to prove his power.) A male or female will show what Jane calls a "full open grin" when frightened or excited, such as when being attacked, or even when spotting a big supply of bananas or other fruit. With this expression, the animal (or a group of animals) will scream loudly with its mouth wide open and teeth flashing. Playful youngsters, such as Fifi when tickling Flint, will put on a "play face," her upper lip pulled back and jaw

Pouting like a child, Fifi sits on a rope and patiently waits for a banana treat from Jane.

slack as she gives little grunts that sound similar to laughing. When a young chimp pouts, it looks much like the pout of a child with its lips pressed together and pushed out. Melissa's tiny Goblin would have done this to let his mother know he needed her or that he was out of sorts. This expression is accompanied by "soft hoo whimpers."

Chimps, Jane noted, are capable of showing great sadness or looking forlorn and bewildered in situations when they are grieving or when they have been captured. (Years later, Jane would grieve as she watched lab chimps who were being mistreated.) All of these signs are indications that chimpanzees, like humans, can express their feelings in many different ways.

One of Jane's earliest discoveries proved that chimpanzees are omnivores—they enjoy meat, fruits, and vegetables, as well as insects and an occasional bird's egg. Through the years, Jane and her associates at the research center have catalogued "more than 90 different species of trees and plants. In their widely varied diet, chimps also enjoy more than 50 kinds of fruit and at least 30 types of leaves and buds as well as blossoms, seeds, tree bark and even fibers from dead wood." Among their favorite insects, chimps will fish for termites, ants, and caterpillars in addition to the grubs, or larvae, of beetles, wasps, and bees. (They love honey!)

Chimpanzees hunt cooperatively, just as early humans did, sharing their kill with others in the group. The most frequently sought animals are the infants of the bushbuck, the bushpig, baboons, and the red colobus monkey.

In 1974, a shocking development occurred that proved that chimpanzees and humans share yet another behavior: the ability to wage war. For four terrible years, the chimps of the Kasakela community in Jane's home valley attacked members of a small group that had split off from the Kasakelas. Both males and females were involved, hunting and slaughtering their enemies—many of whom had once been their companions. Later, members of the powerful Kahama community to the south of the reserve came into the conflict.

Old Flo's son, Figan, was a part of it all as well as Melissa's adolescent offspring, Goblin. Other familiar chimps included Mike, now the reigning alpha male, Goliath, Humphrey, and several females Jane had followed for years, including Madame Bee, daughter Honey Bee, and Gigi. Sniff, a lovable young male whom she had known since the early days at Gombe, was trapped between the Kasakelas and the Kahamas, living a lonely existence for more than a year. His loss, like those of others killed in the battle was deeply felt by Jane, who remembered the time that he had adopted and cared for his infant sibling, Sorema, after the death of their mother. (Sadly, however, the infant did not survive.)

The four-year war was brutal. Savage attacks among the communities brought much pain and suffering, just as in human conflicts. Jane wrote of her anguish during that time:

> For so many years I had believed that chimpanzees, while showing uncanny similarities to humans in many ways were, by and large, rather 'nicer' than us. Suddenly I found that under certain circumstances they could be just as brutal, that they also had a dark side to their nature. For several years I struggled to come to terms with this new knowledge.

Among the first victims was an old friend of Jane's. "Goliath, who had been top-ranking before Mike's reign, was always one of the boldest and bravest of the adult males," she recorded when she came upon him after he had been attacked by his former friends.

"He managed to sit, but with difficulty, and as he gazed after his one-time companions he was trembling violently. He cradled one wrist with his other hand as though it was broken, and his body was covered with wounds. The next day we all turned out to search for him but he too vanished without a trace."

What caused the four-year war? Jane and her team noted that each of the chimpanzee communities at Gombe is fiercely competitive and territorial. Chimps straying into forbidden territory are treated as invaders. However, adolescent females frequently move across these boundaries and are safe in a new community if they are sexually attractive to males at the time. But if they remain in that area after giving birth they become a threat to the existing females. Males in each society try to prevent their females from ranging into "foreign" territory. The Gombe team concluded that an adolescent female's departure from her home region might have started the war.

Beginning in 1975, Jane made another startling discovery. For two years, Passion, a female whose strange behavior had been observed since the birth of her first offspring, took part in violent acts of cannibalism with her daughter Pom. Attacking the infants of members of their own community as well as their "enemies," Passion and Pom killed and ate at least ten little ones after snatching them from their mothers.

Although rare acts of cannibalism had taken place before this, there seemed to be no explanation for the well-organized brutality of the mother-daughter terrorists. Today, the answer remains unknown.

STARTLING DISCOVERIES

Like most scientists, Jane believes that a combination of inherited characteristics and early childhood experiences contribute to individual differences in chimps as well as in people. Commenting on the contrast between the way old Flo treated her young and Passion's attitude toward her daughter Pom, she reminds us that Flo was a patient and affectionate mother who had a loving relationship with each of her offspring. Passion, on the other hand, was completely opposite. She had no close relationships with any of the other females in the community and "was a cold mother, intolerant and brusque, and she seldom played with her infant . . . [Pom] had a difficult time during her early months, and she became an anxious and clinging child, always fearful that her mother would go off and leave her behind."

As two youngsters growing up at the same time, Flo's daughter Fifi and Passion's daughter Pom had very different childhoods. With Flo as a fine role model, Fifi grew into adolescence and adulthood secure and self-confident. As a result, she became a wonderful mother and was as highly regarded in the community as Flo had always been. Pom, with all of her childhood scars, became the "notorious" individual Jane and her team believed her to be. "Pom, after her mother's death, became increasingly solitary and eventually left the community for good."

Flo's nurturing benefited other offspring as well. Her son Figan eventually rose to become "the most powerful alpha male in Gombe's recorded history." And Faben had the emotional and physical strength to cope with living after being severely paralyzed by polio.

Near the end of her life, old Flo became increasingly feeble and had great difficulty getting around. One morning, she was found lying face down in a nearby mountain stream. "Although I had long known the end was close," Jane wrote, "this did nothing to [ease] the grief that filled me . . . I had known her for eleven years and I had loved her."

Three weeks after his mother's death, the dependent young Flint, "hollow-eyed, gaunt and utterly depressed, [died at] the very place where Flo's body had lain."

CHAPTER SEVEN

THE KIDNAPPING

Eight years after the Gombe Research Centre was established, close to twenty students from around the world were observing and collecting information about Jane Goodall's chimpanzees. Some of them were graduate students working in the fields of ethology, anthropology, and psychology. Several of the young men and women were researching the behavior of baboons living side by side with the chimps. A group of Stanford University undergraduates had arrived, as well as zoology majors from the University of Dar es Salaam in Tanzania.

Thatched-roof aluminum huts served as modest living quarters for the young people and a stone and cement mess hall on the shores of Lake Tanganyika was the evening gathering place for everyone including Jane, Hugo, and little Grub—the nickname for Hugo Eric Louis van Lawick, their five-year-old son.

Jane, Hugo, and Grub together on the shores of Lake Tanganyika

The students were enthusiastic about their work and had grown increasingly fond of the fascinating creatures they were observing. "There were weekly seminars at which we discussed research findings and planned ever better ways of [comparing] the information from the various studies," Jane noted. "There was a spirit of cooperation . . . a willingness to share data."

Individual files were kept on each chimp and records of "follows," which sometimes lasted for a month or more, helped to explain changes in behavior or to note the curious differences between one chimp and another. One study involved a fifty-five-day follow of Melissa, who had given birth to twins—a rare occurrence in the chimpanzee world.

Jane's life was busier now than ever before. Having earned her Ph.D. at Cambridge, she spent three months each year teaching a course in human biology at Stanford University in California. At home in Gombe she devoted much time to caring for her son, a little boy who thrived in the natural environment in which he lived.

NIGHT OF TERROR

One dark night in May 1975, the Gombe Research Centre was invaded by terrorists. Forty armed gunmen from the neighboring country of Zaire

Melissa with her twins, Gyre and Gimble

crossed Lake Tanganyika in search of American students to kidnap and hold for ransom. Four young people were seized. As the kidnappers moved off with their hostages, two African women who had been awakened by the commotion raced through the darkness to spread the news of the attack.

In May 1975 came a sudden night of terror.

Jane—by now married to her second husband, Derek Bryceson—fled with the other young people to Dar es Salaam. Fearing for the lives of the captured students, she waited anxiously for word from the kidnappers. A week later, one student was returned with a note demanding a ransom for the remaining captives.

The reasons for the kidnappings were political and the negotiations between the three countries involved (the United States, Tanzania, and Zaire) continued for almost two months. Concerned for the safety of the young Americans and having no idea of their location, Jane and Derek felt helpless.

Time dragged on endlessly. At last, word reached Dar es Salaam that an agreement had been reached. With the payment of a ransom, two more students were freed. Two weeks later, the last remaining hostage was released.

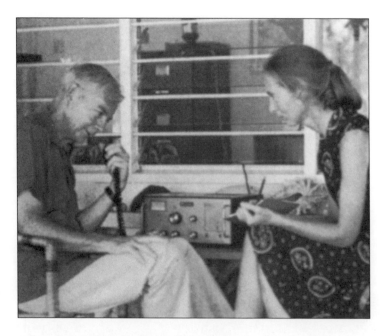

Jane and Derek, from their home in Dar es Salaam, kept in touch with Gombe through the use of a two-way radio.

Years later, Jane would write about those dark weeks and the nightmares she experienced long after the crisis had passed. "Without Derek's help and support I doubt that I could have maintained Gombe after the kidnapping."

Introduced to Derek Bryceson in 1973 while visiting friends in Dar es Salaam, Jane found that she and the Englishman immediately liked each other. After her marriage to Derek, Jane's responsibilities for daily record keeping were turned over to her increasingly capable African staffers. In the weeks following the release of the hostages, it was agreed that the young people were no longer safe at Gombe and that they should return home. Jane was spending most of her time at Dar es Salaam, working on a book based upon her scientific research. Sadly, the couple had only five years together before Derek's death of cancer in 1980.

CHAPTER EIGHT

GOMBE AND BEYOND: THE WORK CONTINUES

Almost forty years have passed since Jane Goodall began her study of the chimpanzees of Gombe Stream. During that time she has observed humans' closest living relatives as they live in their wilderness world, raising their young and fighting for a place in their unique and complex society. Looking back over those years, Jane has fond memories of gentle David Greybeard, the first of the chimps to trust her presence, and Old Flo, the role model mother who taught her the importance of good parenting. At Gombe, Jane witnessed the suffering of animals afflicted with human diseases, and marveled at the loyalty between individuals like Figan and his paralyzed brother Faben, a polio victim. Each of these chimps, and many others, occupy a special place in her heart.

As time passes, new discoveries about the way chimps live have come to light because of Jane's work. The world now knows that the animals can make tools and wage war, that individuals are capable of great emotion and can feel joy, fear, and sorrow just as humans can. We have also learned that chimps depend on each other for companionship and support.

Jane's work continues at Gombe through the efforts of a devoted staff. Observations have proven that chimpanzees use certain plants as medicine to cure stomachaches and to reduce internal parasites. In another development, Mel, a sickly little orphan male whose mother had died of pneumonia, was adopted by Spindle, an adolescent who shared his nest and his food with him. And in 1995, a chimp named Rafiki gave birth to Roots and Shoots, marking only the second time in more than thirty-five years that twins have been born at Gombe Stream.

Today, one of Jane Goodall's major concerns is the spread of the human population. Human development is rapidly closing in on Gombe National Park and other parts of the equatorial forest that stretches across Africa.

When Jane arrived at Gombe in 1960, "there may have been as many as ten thousand chimpanzees living in Tanzania, while today there can be no more than two thousand five hundred," she

One of Jane's main concerns is the welfare of chimpanzees in captivity. Here, during a 1995 visit to the Brazzaville Zoo in the Congo, she is groomed by Grégoire.

says. Thanks to government protection, however, the chimps there are luckier than in other parts of the forest belt.

Once, the chimpanzees of Africa numbered in the hundreds of thousands, living in as many as twenty-five countries. In four of those nations the animals are now extinct and the populations in the others have been alarmingly reduced.

With the spread of the human population, forests are being cleared for housing and farming. Mining and logging continues to expand. The spread of human diseases, so easily caught by the chimps, has cost the lives of countless numbers. One of the worst problems facing the animals in West and Central Africa is the capture of infant chimpanzees for food, entertainment, or use as pets. Mothers trying to protect their young are frequently shot or poisoned.

"The whole sickening business of capturing infant chimpanzees, for any purpose whatsoever, is not only cruel but also horribly wasteful," Jane tells people. "Often the youngsters as well as the mothers are hit . . . and if other chimpanzees rush to the defense of the mother and her child, then they may be shot also." Most shocking of all is the fact that for every animal who survives transportation into captivity, ten to twenty others may have died.

In 1986, Jane Goodall began speaking out against these inhumane practices. Since then, she has traveled throughout Africa and the rest of the world to let people know about the plight of these remarkable animals. In addition to her lectures and best-selling books she has campaigned against the cruelty to animals living in zoos and the vast numbers that are being used in laboratory testing for AIDS, hepatitis, and other diseases.

When Dr. Goodall is not at Gombe Research Centre, she leaves it in the capable hands of two researchers: Anthony Collins, Director of Baboon Research, and Dr. Shadrack Kamenya, Director of Chimpanzee Research. They are assisted by videographer Bill Wallauer and an international staff of scientists, students, and field-workers.

The chimpanzees need our help now more than ever before, and we can only help if we each do our bit, no matter how small it may seem.

Jane logs thousands of miles of air travel each year to promote the work of the Jane Goodall Institute, an organization dedicated to the welfare of animals in the wild (particularly chimpanzees), environmental research, conservation, and education. Thanks to her efforts and the interest of thousands of committed people, the Institute has set up branches in the United States, Great Britain, Canada, Germany, Tanzania, and the Republic of Congo. To promote her work, Jane makes several trips to the United States each year. She meets with members of Congress, holds press conferences, and appears on television programs, including *Nightline, Good Morning America, National Geographic Explorer,* and *Nature Watch.*

What caused Jane Goodall to begin campaigning for the welfare of chimpanzees? It all began when Jane was sent a videotape of a testing lab in Rockville, Maryland, where the animals were being injected with disease vaccines for the National Institutes of Health. The conditions at the lab were horrible. Infant chimps sat rocking back and forth in tiny cages so cramped that they could hardly move.

"We all sat watching the tape, and we were all shattered," Jane recalled as she described what she saw.

Soon after, an investigation of the lab and its records proved that the chimps were being held in filthy cages where they were inadequately fed and often without water. In March 1987, Jane visited the lab and was horrified. Describing the chimps later in the book *Visions of Caliban*, she wrote of their eyes, "dull and blank, like the eyes of people who have lost all hope . . ."

Five years later, lab director John Landon thanked Jane for speaking out against him. "I could have strangled you . . . but now I want to show you what we have done." Returning to the facility, Jane found spacious new cages with climbing poles and sleeping platforms. No longer alone, the chimps now keep company in pairs and are allowed to play with lab workers.

Although improvements like these are encouraging, Jane knows that her campaign must continue. "Of course I should like to see all lab cages standing empty, but as long as it is thought necssary for animals to be used in labs, they should be given the most humane treatment possible, and the best living conditions," she explains.

In addition to traveling and lecturing, Jane's tireless efforts to improve living conditions for chimpanzees have resulted in programs that encourage people of all ages to become better informed about the plight of these wonderful creatures. Under the sponsorship of the Jane Goodall Institute, sanctuaries providing long-term care for orphaned chimps have been established at six different locations in Africa. "Wildlife Awareness" weeks held in Burundi, Sierra Leone, Congo, and other African nations teach through films, school

Jane discusses Roots & Shoots during a visit with schoolchildren in Connecticut. "Teaching them to care for the earth, and each other, is our hope for the future," she says.

visitations, wildlife walks, lectures, and fund-raising dinners. "Roots & Shoots," named in honor of Jane's philosophy on the power of young people to make a difference, encourages environmental awareness and community involvement. (The twins born at Gombe in 1995 were named after this program.) ChimpanZoo works to promote the study of chimpanzees living in zoos and other captive settings throughout the world.

As Jane Goodall reminds us, "Every individual matters. Every individual has a role to play. Every individual makes a difference!"

CHRONOLOGY

1934	Jane Goodall is born in London, England, on April 3.
1935	Jane is given "Jubilee," the chimpanzee toy that starts a lifelong love of animals.
1937	The "little naturalist" is discovered missing.
1938	Judy, Jane's sister, is born.
1938–40	Jane revels in exploring the wildlife around her home in Bournemouth.
1942	Jane begins to dream of living with the animals in Africa.
1942–54	Jane's school years continue.
1955	Jane works in a London film studio that produces documentaries.
1956	Jane receives an invitation to visit a friend in Africa. She returns to Bournemouth to earn money for her journey to Africa.
1957	Jane arrives at Mombasa, Kenya, East Africa and is soon introduced to the famous anthropologist, Dr. Louis Leakey.
1957–58	Working as Dr. Leakey's secretary at the National Museum of Natural History, Jane

joins Louis and his wife Mary in their archaeological excavations at Olduvai Gorge, East Africa. Soon after, Jane agrees to study the chimpanzees of Gombe Stream.

1958–60   Jane returns to England while Dr. Leakey works to raise funds to support her study of the Gombe chimpanzees.

1960   Jane and her mother Vanne arrive at Gombe in June. In September, they are stricken with malaria. They recover, and Jane gets her first glimpse of the secretive chimpanzees in December.

1961   Jane Goodall makes two important discoveries that change the way scientists think about chimpanzee behavior. Other important discoveries quickly follow as the animals lose their shyness. Vanne returns to England, and Dr. Leakey arranges for Jane to study animal behavior at Cambridge University in England. Dominic and Hassan continue the Gombe Stream research in her absence.

1962   Hugo van Lawick arrives to photograph the Gombe chimps in August. Jane returns to Gombe from Cambridge. New discoveries continue and the Gombe camp expands. By December, Jane is planning for her new term at Cambridge University.

1963   Jane continues her studies at Cambridge.

1964   Jane and Hugo marry and return to Gombe together.

1965   The National Geographic Society provides funding for new buildings and a small staff.

1966	Tragedy strikes when polio afflicts many Gombe chimps.
1967	The Gombe Stream Reserve becomes the Gombe National Park, protected by the African government. Research continues, and Jane completes her Ph.D studies. She continues to make new discoveries at Gombe and accepts invitations to lecture abroad.
1970	A son, Hugo Eric Louis van Lawick, is born to Jane and Hugo.
1972	University students arrive from several countries to study the Gombe chimps.
1974	Jane reports the following disturbing discoveries: A four-year war begins among the Gombe chimps, and researchers witness cannibalism practiced by Passion and her offspring Pom. Later, Jane and Hugo divorce.
1975	Jane marries Derek Bryceson. In May, terrorists from neighboring Zaire invade the camp and take several students hostage. After two weeks of anguish, the kidnapped students are released.
Today	Dr. Goodall's work on behalf of animal welfare continues to have an impact throughout the world.

In gathering materials for the writing of *Jane Goodall: Pioneer Researcher*, I was fortunate to have access to the Jane Goodall Institute (listed in the For More Information section of this book), which served as an excellent font of information and will be of great value to readers wanting to know more about this remarkable woman's work. Many sources are available through the National Geographic Society, which has sponsored Dr. Goodall's research from its beginnings in the early 1960s. Articles by and about Jane Goodall that have appeared in National Geographic since that time are lively and fun to read, offering timely insight into the nature and habits of chimpanzees—our closest living relatives in the world of apes.

Two of Dr. Goodall's books, *In the Shadow of Man* and *Through a Window*, offer readers the opportunity to explore the scientist's innermost feelings as she laid the groundwork for her revolutionary research of the chimpanzees. They are personal accounts that allow readers a chance to learn more about Goodall's private experiences and her passion for her work. In *Walking with the Great Apes*, readers will discover the striking similarities among chimpanzees, gorillas, and orangutans, as seen through the eyes of Goodall, Dian Fossey (*Gorillas in the Mist*), and Birute Galdikas, a pioneer in the studies of the orangutans of Borneo.

Young people wanting to get involved in Jane Goodall's efforts to protect the wild chimpanzees and to ensure the welfare of those used in lab research can contact the Jane Goodall Institute for Wildlife Research, Education and Conservation. Students may want to become (individually or as a class) guardians of chimpanzees now living in African sanctuaries that have been established by the institute. Information about these programs can be found in the For More Information section of this book.

FOR MORE INFORMATION

BOOKS BY JANE GOODALL

Chimpanzees. Atheneum, 1989.
In the Shadow of Man. Houghton Mifflin, 1971. (Photographs by Hugo van Lawick.)
Through a Window. Houghton Mifflin, 1990.
Visions of Caliban. Houghton Mifflin, 1993.
My Friends the Wild Chimpanzees. National Geographic Society, 1967.

BOOKS ABOUT JANE GOODALL AND AFRICA

Ferber, Elizabeth. *Jane Goodall: A Life with Animals*. Benchmark Books, 1997.
Fromer, Julie. *Jane Goodall: Living with the Chimps*. 21st Century Books, 1992.
Montgomery, Sy. *Walking with the Great Apes*. Houghton Mifflin, 1991.
Pratt, Paula B. *Jane Goodall*. Lucent Books, 1996.

Regan, Colm and Pedar Cremin. *Africa.* Raintree Steck-Vaughn, 1997.

The Great Apes: Between Two Worlds. Contributions by Jane Goodall, George B. Schaller and Mary G. Smith. National Geographic Society, 1993.

MAGAZINE ARTICLES BY AND ABOUT JANE GOODALL

"A Curious Kinship: Apes and Humans." National Geographic Society, March 1992.

"Crusading for Chimps and Humans . . . Jane Goodall." National Geographic Society, December 1995.

"Jane Goodall at Gombe: A 30th Anniversary." National Geographic Society, August 1990.

"Life and Death at Gombe." National Geographic Society, May 1979.

"My Life Among Wild Chimpanzees." National Geographic Society, August 1963.

"New Discoveries Among Africa's Chimpanzees." National Geographic Society, December 1965.

"Wild Chimps' Status to Be Ruled Endangered." National Geographic Society, August 1989.

ORGANIZATIONS AND INTERNET RESOURCES

Discovering Chimps
http://www.biosci.cbs.umn.edu/chimp/index.html
Sponsored by the Jane Goodall Institute for Primate Studies and the University of Minnesota, this site

studies the ecology, evolution, and behavior of chimpanzees and other primates.

The Jane Goodall Institute for Wildlife Research, Education and Conservation
P.O. Box 14890
Silver Spring, MD 20911
E-mail: jgi@gsn.org
http://www.gsn.org/project/jgi/index.html
At the Institute's home page, you can learn more about available youth and education programs, Roots & Shoots, and how you or your class can adopt a captive chimpanzee.

The Jane Goodall Center for Excellence in Environmental Studies
http://www.wcsu.ctstateu.edu/cyberchimp/homepage.html
Here you'll find information about Jane Goodall, the Gombe Stream Research Centre and Chimpanzee Sanctuaries, color photographs of Jane and her chimpanzees, the latest news from the Gombe Stream Research Centre, and links to chimpanzee-related sites.

Jane Goodall Research Centre
http://www.usc.edu/dept/elab/anth/goodall.html
Students can use this site to pursue virtual study of the animals at Gombe.

Jane Goodall: The Great Conservationist
http://www.simplecom.net/jbindon/jane_goodall.htm
Found on Excite, this site links you to several related

sites. Included is an in-depth look at Jane Goodall's work on behalf of animals and an explanation of how unusual it was for a woman to go into the African wilderness for an intensive scientific study. You can also meet the chimpanzees of Gombe and learn how Jane's research techniques became the model for wildlife observation throughout the world.

Center for Captive Chimpanzee Care
P.O. Box 3746
Boynton Beach, FL 33424
E-mail: info@savethechimps.org
http://www.savethechimps.org
Jane Goodall is one of the directors of this center, which seeks to inform the public about the problems and struggles experienced by captive chimpanzees, particularly those used in medical experiments. Included are color photos of chimpanzees and links to other sites.

INDEX

Page numbers in *italics* indicate illustrations.

ABOUT THE AUTHOR

Jayne Pettit has written numerous books for young people, including *My Name is San Ho* (Scholastic, 1992), *A Place to Hide: True Stories of the Holocaust* (Scholastic, 1993 and Macmillan, 1994), *A Time to Fight Back: True Stories of Children's Resistance During WW II* (Macmillan, 1994 and Houghton Mifflin, 1995), and *Journey of the Heart: The Story of Maya Angelou* (Dutton, 1996 and Penguin, 1998).

Mrs. Pettit holds an MA Ed. degree and has taught in the public and independent school sector for seventeen years. She is the mother of three grown children, the grandmother of seven, and lives with her husband on Hilton Head Island, South Carolina.